W9-CFB-402

Sports Illustrated KIDS

REAL HEROES OF SPORTS
HEROES UNDER PRESSURE

BY HANS HETRICK

CAPSTONE PRESS
a capstone imprint

Sports Illustrated Kids Stats & Stories are published by Capstone Press,
1710 Roe Crest Drive, North Mankato, Minnesota 56003.
www.mycapstone.com

Copyright © 2017 by Capstone Press, a Capstone imprint. All rights reserved. No part
of this publication may be reproduced in whole or in part, or stored in a retrieval
system, or transmitted in any form or by any means, electronic, mechanical,
photocopying, recording, or otherwise, without written permission of the publisher.

Sports Illustrated Kids is a trademark of Time Inc. Used with permission.

Library of Congress Cataloging-in-Publication Data
Hetrick, Hans, 1973- author.
Title: Heroes under pressure / by Hans Hetrick.
Description: North Mankato, Minnesota : An imprint of Capstone Press, [2017]
  | Series: Sports Illustrated Kids. Real Heroes of Sports. | Includes
  bibliographical references and index. | Audience: Ages: 8-14. | Audience:
  Grades: 4 to 6.
Identifiers: LCCN 2016038718| ISBN 9781515744351 (Library Binding) | ISBN
  9781515744474 (Paperback) | ISBN 9781515744603 (eBook (PDF))
Subjects: LCSH: Sports--Psychological aspects. | Athletes--Conduct of life.
Classification: LCC GV706.55 .H47 2017 | DDC 796.01/9--dc23
LC record available at https://lccn.loc.gov/2016038718

Editorial Credits
Nate LeBoutillier, editor; Terri Poburka, designer;
Eric Gohl, media specialist; Gene Bentdahl, production

Photo Credits
Capstone: cover (top left); Getty Images: Bettmann, 16, Boston Globe, 14, Patrick
McDermott, 17 (top), Stringer/AFP, 29, Transcendental Graphics, 9 (top); Library
of Congress: 20, 21; Newscom: akg-images, 23, EPA/Bernd Thissen, 15, Sipa USA/
Fotoarena, 12, TNS/Jose Carlos Fajardo, 28 (bottom), ZUMA Press/Keystone Pictures
USA, 22, ZUMA Press/Scott Mc Kiernan, 13; Shutterstock: Aleksandr Sulga, cover
(bottom left), 1, Gocili, cover (bottom right), kstudija, cover (top right); Sports
Illustrated: David E. Klutho, 24, 25 (all), 27 (bottom), Hy Peskin, 27 (top), John Biever,
18, John G. Zimmerman, 7, 26, John Iacono, 17 (bottom), 19, Simon Bruty, 10, 11 (all),
28 (top), Tony Triolo, 5, 9 (bottom), Walter Iooss Jr., 6, 8

Design Elements: Shutterstock

Printed in the United States of America.
010054S17

Table of
CONTENTS

INTRODUCTION

Real heroes of sports are forged under pressure. They rise up when the stakes are high. Heroes fight hard and finish strong when their muscles ache and their breath is short. They give clutch performances when the outcome is on the line. Heroes soar despite the immense weight of history. They win when the eyes of the world are upon them. They shine in the shadows of hatred and injustice. They finish their quests in the face of those who believe they don't belong.

The athletes in *Heroes Under Pressure* have proven their excellence under difficult circumstances. Their stories have inspired people all around the world to stay strong when the pressure is on.

Hank
AARON:
Hammering
Out a Legend

   While Hank Aaron chased Babe Ruth's all-time home run record in 1973, he received more mail than anyone in America. More than 3,000 letters a day poured in to Aaron. Many of those letters, however, were filled with hateful messages because Aaron was African-American. Some letters were direct death threats. "You are (not) going to break this record established by the great Babe Ruth if I can help it," one letter read. "My gun is watching your every black move." Some letters even threatened Aaron's children. The FBI started going through his mail and investigating the more dangerous threats.

When the hate mail was reported in the press, thousands upon thousands of positive letters poured in. Fans at away games gave "Hammerin' Hank" standing ovations. But as the 1973 season wore on, Aaron was never without a bodyguard. He couldn't stay in the same hotels as his Atlanta Braves teammates. His parents were often harassed in Aaron's hometown of Mobile, Alabama, and his college-aged daughter received kidnapping threats. Chasing baseball's most sacred record, for the 39-year-old Aaron, was an experience filled with loneliness and fear.

Aaron finished the 1973 season with 713 home runs, one shy of the record, which had stood since Ruth retired in 1935. In his first at-bat of the 1974 season, Aaron hit a home run to tie Ruth. Home run number 715 came three games later on April 8, 1974, in front of a sold out crowd in Atlanta. In the fourth inning, Aaron drove a pitch from the Los Angeles Dodgers' Al Downing deep over the left field wall. As Aaron rounded the bases, legendary sportscaster Vin Scully famously described the scene, saying, "What a marvelous moment for the country and the world. A black man is getting a standing ovation in the Deep South for breaking a record of an all-time baseball idol."

Aaron was given a microphone moments after smashing the homer. He spoke only one sentence to the crowd, saying, "I just thank God it's all over with."

SOLID AS A STONE

Toni Stone was the first woman to play in the Negro Leagues, and she was no joke. As a second baseman for the Indianapolis Clowns in 1953, Stone hit .243 in 50 games.

Hank Aaron launches the homer that topped Babe Ruth.

Carli LLOYD:
One-Woman Wrecking Ball

Carli Lloyd had excelled under pressure before. In both the 2008 and 2012 Olympics, the mid-fielder for the United States Women's National Team had scored gold medal-winning goals. But in the 2015 World Cup, Lloyd failed to score in the first three games. Some critics wondered if she'd lost her touch.

Lloyd answered those critics by turning into a one-woman wrecking ball for the U.S. team. She was brilliant in a semifinal upset over Germany, scoring a goal and assisting on the game-winner. In the finals against Japan, Lloyd became a bona fide U.S. sports hero. She scored an amazing hat trick—three goals—in only 16 minutes' time. Her third goal was an incredible 60-yard chip over the goaltender that was praised as one of greatest goals ever. Lloyd's performance helped the U.S. win its first World Cup in 16 years.

Carli Lloyd (11), in action at the 2015 World Cup

Tim Howard

Heroic FACT

U.S. goalkeeper Tim Howard shattered the World Cup record for saves with 16 in a 2014 World Cup game versus Belgium. Belgium, however, won, 2-1.

Usain
BOLT:
Fastest
Man Alive

At the 2016 Olympics, the "World's Fastest Man" was expected to win gold medals in the 100 meters, 200 meters, and 4 x 100 meter relay. After all, Jamaican sprinter Usain Bolt had done it before. Twice, actually, in the previous two Olympiads.

But sometimes people take talent for granted. What looks like effortlessness when Bolt runs is actually a product of a great mix of elements. Talent is essential, yes. But also important is dedicated training, devotion to a healthy lifestyle, mental perseverance, timing, and even some luck.

Bolt appeared to have bad luck when an injured left hamstring forced him to pull out of the Jamaican Olympic trials in early July of 2016. With the Olympic games just a month away, a full recovery for Bolt seemed unlikely.

But the 29-year-old Bolt indeed rehabilitated the injury and fought off competitors to thrill spectators in three electrifying performances at the Olympic Games in Rio de Janeiro. He pulled off the "triple triple"—three gold medals in three Olympics. His last victory left him feeling relieved. After his final race, an anchor leg of the 4 x 100 meter relay, Bolt said, "I am just happy, proud of myself. It's come true. The pressure is real."

Usain Bolt blows away the competition at the Rio de Janeiro Olympics in 2016.

Kathrine Switzer (261) at the 1967 Boston Marathon

Kathrine
SWITZER:
Outrunning a Myth

At one time, many men believed women shouldn't run marathons. These men were convinced such a grueling activity would lead to unwanted mustaches and enormous legs. Kathrine Switzer never bought into such myths.

The Boston Marathon had been an all-male race for its entire 70-year history when Switzer entered it in 1967. Four miles into the marathon, Switzer was confronted by a race official who charged straight toward her. He swore at Switzer, screaming, "Get out of my race!"

GOOD SAMARITANS

When New Zealand runner Nikki Hamblin tumbled and fell in the 5,000 meter race at the 2016 Olympics, U.S. runner Abbey D'Agostino tripped over her. Showing true Olympic spirit, D'Agostino made sure Hamblin got up and could continue before resuming her run. Soon after, D'Agostino's ankle, injured in the fall, made her collapse. This time, Hamblin stopped to make sure her competitor was okay. While the runners' falls knocked them out of contention, their reactions won them admiration.

Switzer's boyfriend rammed his shoulder into the official and knocked him out of the way. Switzer finished the race in 4:20, ahead of a good number of men. Because of Switzer's determination, the Boston Marathon officially allowed women in 1972.

Abbey D'Agostino (left) and Nikki Hamblin

Charlie
SIFFORD:

Breaking through the "Caucasian Clause"

At 13 years old, Charlie Sifford was a hard-working caddy growing up in North Carolina. In his spare time, he also played the game and was already shooting par. When Sifford came home from World War II, he applied for membership in the Professional Golfers Association (PGA). Because he was African-American, the organization denied his application. But Sifford didn't quit. He played and won tournaments that allowed people of color.

The PGA finally gave him his member card in 1961. Sifford was the first black golfer to earn one. Still, he experienced plenty of hostility on the PGA tour. "I got death threats," said Sifford. "Heard every name in the book. They kicked my ball into traps. I just wanted to show that a black man could play this game and be a gentleman. I did that."

In 2014 Sifford was awarded the Presidential Medal of Freedom. President Barack Obama, the country's first African-American President, bestowed the honor.

President Barack Obama awards the Medal of Freedom to Charlie Sifford in 2014.

Heroic FACT

In 1975 Lee Elder became the first African-American to play The Masters at Augusta. In 1997 Tiger Woods became the first African-American to win The Masters.

Tiger Woods (in red) at The Masters in 1997

Michael
JORDAN:
One Last Bullseye

In 1994 Michael Jordan briefly played minor league baseball in the Chicago White Sox organization.

It took Michael Jordan just 42 seconds to single-handedly secure Game 6 of the 1998 NBA Finals. The Chicago Bulls icon strung together three incredible plays as the clock wound down to zero in the fourth quarter. First, he blew by a defender for a quick layup. Moments later, he swiped the ball from the Utah Jazz's Karl Malone. For the final blow, Jordan drilled a 20-foot game-winning jumper. The shot, Jordan's last as a Bull, gave both Jordan and the Bulls six NBA titles. "We all hopped on Michael's back," teammate Steve Kerr said after the game. "He just carried us. It was his game tonight. That guy was ridiculous."

Five years earlier, that shot seemed impossible. Jordan had retired from basketball in 1993 at age 30 after his beloved father was senselessly murdered. But after 18 months away from professional basketball, Jordan came back to the Bulls. He led the Bulls to titles in 1995–96 and 1996–97 before winning his final title with the Bulls in 1997–98.

Heroic FACT

Despite a severe case of the flu, Michael Jordan somehow scored 38 points to help the Bulls take Game 5 of the 1997 NBA Finals. When the game was over, Jordan collapsed into the arms of teammate Scottie Pippen.

Jesse **OWENS**:

Sprinting Through History

In 1936 Jesse Owens traveled to Germany to compete at the Olympics in front of Adolf Hitler. The Nazi ruler planned to use the 1936 Olympics to showcase the supremacy of his German people. The Nazis believed that blond-haired, blue-eyed Aryans were naturally better than other races. Owens, an African-American sprinter, was there to win gold regardless of the politics of the hosting country. It just so happened that world was watching.

Despite the Nazis' promotion of Aryan racial superiority, the Olympic crowd gathered in Berlin watched in seeming awe rather than disgust. Huge crowds greeted Owens, and he was constantly approached for his autograph. When Owens won the 100-meter dash, the massive crowd erupted with applause.

Owens became the first athlete to win four gold medals in a single Olympics. He might not have done so without the surprising help of a German competitor. In the long jump competition, Owens was in danger of not qualifying for the finals. He had gone over the takeoff line and fouled on his first two jumps. Before his final jump, German long jumper Lutz Long gave Owens some advice. Long suggested that Owens take off on his jump well before the foul line. Owens did so and qualified.

Jesse Owens (center) and Lutz Long (right) on the medal stand at the 1936 Olympics in Berlin, Germany.

In the finals of the long jump, Owens and Long put on a great show. Between them, they topped the Olympic record five times. In the end, Owens took gold with a jump of 26 feet, 5 1/2 inches (8.06 meters) while Long took silver with a mark of 25 feet, 10 inches (7.87 m). When Owens won, Long congratulated him with an embrace—in plain view of Hitler.

"It took a lot of courage for him to befriend me in front of Hitler," Owens later said. "You can melt down all the medals and cups I have, and they wouldn't be a plating on the 24-karat friendship I felt for Lutz Long at that moment."

*Lutz Long and Jesse Owens
in Berlin, 1936*

THE BEST MAN

Lutz Long died in 1943 fighting for Germany in Northern Africa in World War II. Shortly before his death, Long wrote a letter to Jesse Owens. He asked Owens to one day find his son, Karl, and "tell him about how things can be between men on this Earth." Years later, Owens stood at Lutz Long's son's wedding as his best man.

UConn Women's Basketball:
Stunning Domination

Moriah Jefferson

The University of Connecticut women's basketball program has been dominant for years. Since 1994–95, when the program won its first National Collegiate Athletic Association (NCAA) championship, the Huskies have won 10 more titles and never finished a season with fewer than 25 wins.

Between 2012 and 2016, UConn completely dominated the NCAA. Over four seasons, the Huskies posted a 151-5 record and twice finished an entire season undefeated. Each season, they won the NCAA championship. Breanna Stewart, Moriah Jefferson, and Morgan Tuck were the heart of the team. All three were deadly from three-point range. Jefferson could drive by any defender. Stewart and Tuck were unstoppable in the post.

In the 2016 NCAA Tournament, their dominance was especially stunning. They crushed their six opponents by an average of 39.9 points. Stewart, Jefferson, and Tuck were chosen first, second, and third in the 2016 Women's National Basketball Association draft.

Geno
Auriemma

Heroic FACT

UConn coach Geno Auriemma was the head coach of the 2016 Olympic gold medal-winning U.S. Women's basketball team. Five of the 12 Olympic squad's players were UConn alumni.

Breanna Stewart

Ted WILLIAMS:

The Magic Mark of .400

In baseball a .300 batting average is the mark of a fine hitter. A player who hits .400 is considered truly legendary. Going into the last day of the 1941 Major League Baseball season, Boston Red Sox slugger Ted Williams' batting average stood at .39955. Since numbers are rounded up, Williams could have sat out and claimed a monumental .400 season.

The Red Sox were facing the Philadelphia Athletics in a double-header, and Williams insisted on playing. The pressure was on. "I kept thinking about the thousands of swings I had taken to prepare myself," Williams said afterward. "I went to the ballpark more eager to hit than I had ever been."

The Splendid Splinter went 4-for-5 with a home run in the first game, a game in which Boston fell behind 11-3 before pulling out a 12-11 win. In the second game, Boston lost 3-1, but Williams went 2-for-3, raising his season's batting average to a final mark of .406. No hitter has hit .400 or better since.

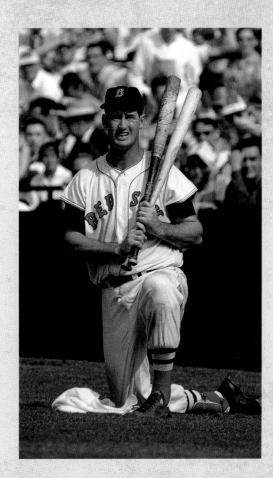

Heroic FACT

The Boston Red Sox stormed back from a three-games-to-none deficit to win the 2004 American League Championship Series over the New York Yankees. Boston then went on the win the World Series, its first championship in 86 years.

LeBron
JAMES:
Promise
Delivered

LeBron James hoists Cleveland's first-ever NBA championship trophy

Cleveland Cavaliers fans were furious when pro hoops superstar LeBron James split for the Miami Heat in 2010. But James, who grew up in nearby Akron, Ohio, returned to Cleveland in 2014 after having won two championships with the Heat. He promised to bring an NBA championship to his hometown team. Cleveland fans cautiously welcomed their former star back. They had been burned by James before. What's more, Cleveland hadn't seen a sports championship of any kind in 50 years.

James delivered on his promise in dramatic fashion in the 2016 NBA Finals. The Cavs stormed back from 3-1 series deficit against the mighty Golden State Warriors. Late in Game 7, James exploded above the rim to block an easy Warrior breakaway layup. The Cavs rode James' heroics to the championship. James' game-changing play will forever be known as "The Block." And Cleveland can never be furious at LeBron James again.

LeBron James makes "The Block."

CLEVELAND, BELIEVELAND

Clevelanders name their sports heartbreaks. There's The Drive, The Fumble, The Shot, The Catch, Red Right 88, The Move, and The Decision. They were all tremendous failures in the city's sporting history. Now, Cleveland has a joyful name on the list: The Block.

Glossary

Aryan – a term used by Nazis to describe a supposed superior race of pure-blooded Germans with blond hair and blue eyes

Caucasian – a person who is of white European descent

clutch – the critical time during a competition when the outcome is at stake

deficit – an amount or score by which someone is losing

dominant – very powerful or important

harrass – to bother and annoy again and again

hostility – anger or unfriendliness

idol – a person who is looked up to or even worshipped

injustice – lack of fairness

perseverance – steadfastness in doing something despite difficulty or delay in achieving success

Read More

Meloche, Renee Taft. *Bethany Hamilton: Riding the Waves.* Heroes for Young Readers. Edmonds, Wash.: YWAM. 2014.

Robinson, Sharon. *Jackie Robinson: American Hero.* New York: Scholastic, 2013.

Stout, Glenn. *Able to Play: Overcoming Physical Challenges* Good Sports. Boston: Houghton Mifflin Harcourt, 2012.

Internet Links

FactHound offers a safe, fun way to find Internet sites related to this book. All of the sites on FactHound have been researched by our staff.

Here's all you do:

Visit *www.facthound.com*

Type in this code: 9781515744351

 Check out projects, games and lots more at
www.capstonekids.com

Index